The Hamelin Incident

A Play

Graham Walker

A SAMUEL FRENCH ACTING EDITION

SAMUEL FRENCH

FOUNDED 1830

SAMUELFRENCH-LONDON.CO.UK
SAMUELFRENCH.COM

CHARACTERS

Narrator
Clerk (Orb)
Angry Lady
Small Man
Tall Man ⎱Townspeople
Big Man, a carter
Red-faced Man, a carpenter⎰
Cowled Figure (Martin)
Mayor (Herr Burgomeister)
Johann Blankenfeld, Town Councillor
Mayor's Wife (Frau Burgomeister)
Doctor
Rollo, a small crippled boy
Piper
Gravell ⎱Town Councillors
Schmidt⎰
1st Rat
2nd Rat
3rd Rat
4th Rat
5th Rat
6th Rat
7th Rat
Townspeople, Children

Prologue

THE HAMELIN INCIDENT

A Light comes up on the Narrator, who is standing downstage

The Narrator can remain on stage throughout the play, or come on and off as required

Narrator Hamelin Town's in Brunswick,
By famous Hanover city;
The River Weser, deep and wide,
Washes its walls on the southern side;
A pleasanter spot you never spied;
But, when begins our ditty,
Almost five hundred years ago,
To see the townsfolk suffer so
From vermin, was a pity.

A scuttling and squeaking is heard; the shadows of rats flicker across the dimly lit stage

Rats!
They fought the dogs and killed the cats,
And bit the babies in the cradles,
And ate the cheese out of the vats,
And licked the soup from the cooks' own ladles,
Split open the kegs of salted sprats,
Made nests inside men's Sunday hats,
 And even spoilt the women's chats
By drowning their speaking
With shrieking and squeaking
In fifty different sharps and flats.

The Lights come up on the Town Clerk's office
A gradually increasing noise of shouting is heard

At last the people in a body
To the Town Hall came flocking. . . .

SCENE 1

The Town Clerk's Office—a sparsely furnished room with two doors, one leading to the Mayor's Parlour and one through which the Townspeople enter

The Clerk sits at a high desk, writing with an impressive looking quill pen. The shouting and hammering reach a peak, and individual voices are heard calling for the Mayor. The Clerk, irritated, gets down from the desk and goes to the door

A crowd of angry Townspeople rushes in, almost bowling over the Clerk

Clerk You can't see the Mayor, I tell you! He's in conference.

Angry Lady Conferences yet! Get him *out* of conference!

Small Man That's right! Get the old windbag out here!

Angry Lady Our children should die while he's in conference.

Tall Man I know his conferences. I brought the pies and puddings for his conference this morning!

Big Man Yes, and I brought two barrels of best Rhenish!

Clerk I tell you he can't be disturbed. It's a most important meeting. The Corporation is discussing . . . the new school.

Angry Lady My life already, what's to discuss in a new school? We're being eaten alive by rats!

Small Man That's right! Our food's being stolen from our mouths!

There is a general shout of "She's right! She's right!"

Tall Man To go in the street is to take your life in your hands. And they're talking about schools!

Angry Lady (*appealing to the rest*) For why should we need schools with the children all dead from rat bites, I ask you?

Tall Man Only this morning my youngest had his cot upset by the brutes. There must have been dozens of them!

Big Man My chickens have all been killed!

Tall Man I only just drove them off in time!

Angry Lady What's next? What's next?

Small Man The geese, I shouldn't wonder!

Big Man Or my horses!

Clerk (*desperately trying to keep the peace*) Townsfolk, good people . . . the Mayor has tried everything to rid the town of these creatures . . .

Red-faced Man Like eating five-course dinners!

Big Man And voting himself a salary increase!

Clerk (*waving his arms*) A reward has been proclaimed; even now the bills are being posted . . .

Angry Lady *More* food for the rats!

There is a general shout of agreement

Clerk It was the Corporation's first increase in five years!

Red-faced Man Except round their bellies!

Small Man Thank God they aren't paid in accordance with their waist measurements! We'd be even more broke than we are.

Clerk Everything possible's being done. But there are other things to attend to. The town doesn't run itself . . .

Red-faced Man We'd be better off if we did! We certainly couldn't do worse!

Angry Lady (*sarcastically*) You wouldn't want them to work for nothing now, would you?

Thin Man Why not? That's all they do, isn't it?

Angry Lady Why *don't* you get the Mayor? My life! It would be easier for me to get an audience with the Pope . . .

Small Man Why's he so shy all of a sudden?

Red-faced Man He wasn't shy at election time!

Big Man If you had his record since then, you'd be shy yourself!

Clerk Citizens . . . good people . . . this kind of talk will get us nowhere . . .

Angry Lady We'll be good citizens when we get a good Mayor!

Tall Man (*holding up his arms for quiet*) No kind of talk gets us anywhere. There's been too much talk. (*He turns to the Clerk*) Now, listen. Here's a reasonable choice: either you go through the door and ask the Mayor to be so good as to step out here, or we'll break it down, and use you as the ram! Now, which is it to be?

Clerk (*fluttering*) Well, I really don't know. . . . Not the proper channels, not the proper channels at all . . . (*Then as Big Man steps forward menacingly*) I'll do what I can. I'll try and persuade his worship to see you . . .

Tall Man (*grimly*) And no tricks! Unless you *like* being locked into burning Town Halls!

The Clerk exits

Small Man There's no doubt, you know, politeness always pays in the end.

Big Man (*puzzled*) I wonder, though, if this will do any good? I mean, being fair, what can the Mayor do that hasn't been tried already?

Thin Man He can give us a fair hearing, for a start!

Red-faced Man It's all right for these officials; they've all got their big houses up on the Koppelberg. They don't know what a plague of rats is like!

Angry Lady (*becoming over-excited*) So many traps I've set, you can't walk in the house for them! Dogs running all over!

Red-faced Man If the Corporation put its boots on and helped stamp a few hundred to death, that would be a start.

Small Man It *would* be something positive.

Angry Lady Positive! We should be so lucky!

Big Man The dogs just run away.

Small Man I know. Can you blame them?

Tall Man (*dejectedly*) I know. It's all but hopeless.

Angry Lady (*waving her arms*) One of the traps the rats even ate —spring and all!

Cowled Figure It is a visitation from God. We have sinned.

Angry Lady Such a big visitation! For such little sins!

Cowled Figure None the less, we are accursed. I see the Figure of Death pointing at Hamelin. I hear the wails, and weeping in the streets.

Thin Man I hear weeping. I hear weeping every night. My children cry themselves asleep because they're so afraid.

Cowled Figure (*softly and sadly*) There will be greater sorrow.

Small Man Well, if there's anything worse to come, I only hope I'm not around to see it!

The door to the Mayor's Parlour opens and the Mayor appears with the nervous Clerk at his elbow. He is an immensely fat man, red in the face and richly dressed. He still has a napkin tucked into his collar and is brushing crumbs from his mouth. He looks distinctly uneasy. Everybody starts shouting at once. Fists are waved. The Clerk waves his own arms desperately, and by degrees silence is restored

Clerk Please . . . please . . . good people . . . honest citizens . . .
Mayor I can't hear if you all shout at once. Now then, what is it? Let one of you speak for the rest.
Angry Lady (*backed by the rest*) He's right!

There are shouts of "He's right!", "Let one speak," etc. and the Thin Man is pushed forward

Mayor That's better. Now, what's on your mind?
Red-faced Man On our minds? What's on our minds? Why, rats, you damned fool, rats! What else could it be?

The cry of "Rats" becomes general, and the meeting threatens once more to disintegrate. The Thin Man raises his arms

Thin Man (*speaking slowly and picking his words with care*) Your Worship must be aware of the plague of rats in the town. They steal our food, they kill our animals, they attack our children. We can't stand no more of it, sir. So we've come to you to ask straight out, what are you going to do?
Red-faced Man You get paid enough!
Small Man Get off your backside for once!
Angry Lady Just what are you doing, yet?
Small Man (*jeeringly*) It's a military secret!
Mayor (*very pompously*) If you insist on behaving with insolence to your betters, it would have been more sensible not to have come at all. I've agreed to hear you at great inconvenience to myself; I insist on being treated with the respect due to my office.
Thin Man (*stung*) I respect any man that knows his trade and does it with a will. As for your office, sir, I wouldn't go on too much about that. We put you into it—
Red-faced Man (*interrupting excitedly*) And we can put you out again!
Angry Lady You watch your step, Herr Burgomeister!
Small Man If this goes on much longer you won't have an office! You'll be back in your butcher's shop trying to sell scrag end for silverside again! Only you won't have no customers!

There is a general roar of approval. The Mayor backs off a little, now looking positively alarmed. The Thin Man once more makes himself heard

Thin Man The thing is, Herr Burgomeister, what *are* you and the Corporation doing? We want some straight answers; we've waited long enough.

Mayor (*attempting to regain control of the situation*) We've . . . ah . . . well, we've—I—have appointed a Rat Control Sub-committee. With . . . ah . . . full powers to take any action they think fit. We've advertised a reward of two thousand guilders, payable from our own pockets, to anyone who can rid the town of these creatures. I am concerned, naturally, we are all concerned. Everything possible is being done!

Red-faced Man (*drawing a paper from his pocket*) Well, it so happens we've brought along a few ideas of our own. (*He reads*) "We demand the instant allocation of money from the rates for the purchase of more dogs. We demand the instant formation of paid bands of citizens for the purpose of locating and exterminating nests. We demand a bounty, payable by the Health Inspector, for every dead rat brought to him. We demand the issue of free traps to every household. We demand—"

Mayor (*aghast*) Stop! For Heaven's sake, stop! This is ridiculous. You just don't seem to realize, the town's broke. The rats have cost us so much already we're even having to borrow the money for the reward. There isn't anything left . . .

Big Man You seem to have kept back enough to see yourselves through in food and drink!

Mayor (*smoothly, beginning to regain some confidence*) Oh, no, my friend, you're quite wrong there. The victuals you helped deliver here are for distribution to the poor and needy. We were meeting when you arrived to discuss—ah—the fairest way of making the handout.

Big Man (*taken aback*) Well . . . maybe I was hasty . . .

Red-faced Man Are you mad? Poor and needy! The next time he thinks about the poor and needy will be the first! (*He turns on his heel*) Well, I've said my piece and I'm off. But I warn you—(*pointing at the Mayor*)—you and the whole idle Corporation: get some results, and get them soon, or you're out. Sacked—finished. The whole pack of you!

Angry Lady That goes for all of us!
Small Man The party's over. It's the rats or you!

The Townspeople exit, muttering among themselves

Thin Man (*turning back in the doorway*) This is our last word. We'll give you twenty-four hours—just twenty-four hours. After that, watch for your lives. The rats haven't bitten through the lamp-posts yet, and I've got a yard or two of rope!

The Thin Man goes out
The Mayor sinks into the Clerk's chair, wiping his face

Mayor Phew, thank Heavens that's over! Why did you let in that rabble in the first place?
Clerk (*anxiously*) I did my best, Your Worship. But they just pushed past me. They were very angry . . .
Mayor It's not their place to be angry. It's their place to pay their taxes and keep out of my Town Hall . . . Well, I've got rid of them this time. But they'll be back, you mark my words. And what are we going to do then, I should like to know . . .

Blankenfeld, an official of the Town Council, enters. He is an honest, open man, deeply distressed by the troubles of the town

Mayor Ah, Blankenfeld, you might be able to help. You have more to do with this scum than I have. Threatening me, in my own Town Hall. Can't you reason with them? Make them see their place?
Blankenfeld (*earnestly*) They aren't unreasonable folk, Your Worship. But if you were to see, as I see every day, what they're putting up with . . . There are no rats in your great house; they'd need wings to get there. But down in the city, in my own home . . . Rats in every cupboard, rats on every shelf. Rats in every box, in the larder, in the pantry, in the cheese casks, in the butter. Rats in the attics, in the nurseries, pattering all night like squalls of rain . . .
Mayor (*unsympathetically*) You could always move out. You aren't all that hard up.
Blankenfeld (*quietly and with dignity*) I feel them to be my people. I must share their hardship.
Mayor (*exploding*) *Your* people! Good God, man, what sort of talk is that? That slogan-hurling rabble? They're no better

than the rats they're complaining about. You'll be telling me
next they appreciate your living amongst them. Well, I'll tell
you something: they don't.

*The Clerk hurries forward with his hat and cloak. The Mayor rises
and continues his homily while adjusting them*

They probably resent you all the more for it. When you've
been in public service as long as I have, you'll learn to face a
few home-truths about your precious working classes. And
this is one of 'em: that equality is decided from beneath, not
from above. They don't want your charity, Blankenfeld; they
don't want your good works; and they don't want *you*!

*The Mayor's Wife enters. Frau Burgomeister is a large florid
person: she looks in fact what she is, a butcher's wife raised
above her station. The Mayor doesn't look at all pleased to see
her*

Ah, my dear, I was just on the point of departing. Is our coach
ready?

Wife Ready and waiting this last half-hour. Really, Otto, it's
too bad of you. You *know* we have the Kempenfelds to dinner
this evening, and here you are still messing about in this grubby
old office . . .

*The Clerk begins to grin; the expression is smothered hastily as
the Mayor turns on him his baleful eye*

Mayor See you get those papers finished before you go!

Clerk (*obsequiously*) Yes, sir, of course. Certainly, sir, at once.
I do *hope* Your Worship has a pleasant evening.

Wife (*noticing Blankenfeld for the first time*) Herr Blankenfeld,
is it not? And how *is* that little boy of yours? A sweet child,
such a tragedy . . . *Otto!*

*The Mayor's Wife sweeps out without waiting for an answer, or
indeed without giving Blankenfeld a chance to speak. The Mayor
trots obediently after her*

Clerk (*sighing*) What a fine thing it must be to be a Mayor. And
married to such a fine, upstanding lady as the Frau Burgomeister!

Blankenfeld (*wryly*) Orb, have you been at the decanter again?
Come on, I'll help you with those papers . . .

*Blankenfeld and the Clerk move towards the desk, as the Lights
fade to a Black-out and—*

the CURTAIN *falls*

A Light shines on the Narrator, who is standing downstage as before

Narrator So up to the hills the Mayor went,
    Only on pleasure was he bent.
    Down through a darkening Hamelin Street
    Blankenfeld moves through the evening heat.
    His son to the Doctor he must meet
    To look again at his crooked feet,
    Damaged by a simple game,
    Must he for ever stumble, lame?

SCENE 2

The Doctor's Surgery

*The Doctor, an elderly man with a trim grey beard, is sitting at his
desk. As the Lights come up, he is giving a pot of ointment to the
Small Man, who is sitting on the other side of the desk*

Doctor Rub that on the arm twice a day and it will draw the
inflammation. You should soon be feeling easier.

Small Man Thank you, Herr Doctor. (*He gets up and moves
towards the door*)

*Blankenfeld enters with his small son Rollo, who walks with the
aid of a crutch*

Small Man Herr Blankenfeld, good evening! What brings you
here? Don't tell me you've been bitten by a rat as well?

Blankenfeld No, Ernst, we are giving the Herr Doctor another
problem for a change.

Small Man (*uncomfortably, looking at Rollo*) Well, I've no doubt
he'll soon have that right. Good luck anyway. And good-bye.

Blankenfeld Good night, Ernst.

Rollo Good night, Herr Schmid.

The Small Man exits

Doctor (*rising from the desk; affably*) Good evening, Johann. Hello, Rollo. Now, if I might just have a look at that leg . . . Sit over here. Now, if we just roll down your stocking a moment . . . hmm . . .

The Doctor bends over the boy for a moment while Blankenfeld stands by waiting anxiously

Doctor (*smiling*) That will be all, Rollo, thank you. Now why don't you go along to the kitchen and have a word with Cook? If you're extra polite to her she might even give you some of those cakes she baked an hour ago.

Rollo (*looking pleased*) Thank you, Herr Doctor!

Rollo exits

Blankenfeld Well, Doctor, let's hear the worst.

Doctor (*sighing*) I'm afraid it doesn't look very good, Johann. There's no improvement; the muscles have wasted and there's permanent damage to the tendons. He'll never walk without a crutch again.

Blankenfeld (*shaking his head*) I feared as much. And he was always so keen on games, and running. He was never still.

Doctor Normally, a broken limb in a youngster mends as good as new, but just once in a while . . . I'm sorry, Johann. It's very bad luck.

Blankenfeld It's God's will, I suppose. (*He shakes his head again*) I try not to be ungrateful, but sometimes the world seems such an unfair place. Why should a child like Rollo suffer all his days for a simple slip, when all round us the wicked go unpunished?

Doctor I think it's not for us to judge. There is a justice Johann —a High Justice, beyond our understanding. (*He smiles a little wryly*) Besides, think what a boring world it would be if each sin received its punishment as soon as committed! I like to think of the Lord as more than a sort of cosmic tally clerk!

Blankenfeld (*smiling in turn*) I think our Mayor was wondering just which of the Corporation's sins brought the plague of rats,

Doctor Yes, well he may. Is anything being done, Johann? Anything at all? It's getting worse by the hour in the town.

Blankenfeld Everything we can think of has been tried. I think the Herr Burgomeister is at his wits' end. I know I am.

Doctor Well, he'd best think up something effective before election time. The people won't stand much more.

Blankenfeld I know. There was a deputation at the Town Hall today. He even interrupted his lunch to talk to them. You can see how seriously he must be taking it!

Rollo enters, holding a bag of cakes

Rollo Fraulein Krauf's cakes are really good, Father! I ate two, and she gave me these to take away.

Blankenfeld Did she indeed! Well, I hope you remembered to thank her properly . . .

The Cowled Figure enters softly

Doctor Good evening, Martin. Have you brought the herbs?

The Cowled Figure holds out a basket which the Doctor takes

Cowled Figure From the banks of the Weser.

Doctor (*looking into the basket*) When the good Lord made earth and the green things upon it, He placed His mark on each, so we might know it and which of our human ills it would best cure. We have much to thank Him for . . . Martin, have you met Herr Blankenfeld here and Rollo?

Cowled Figure Only in my dreams. (*He bows*)

Doctor Martin has the gift of dreams and prophecy. He knows the future.

Blankenfeld And what does the future hold for Hamelin?

Cowled Figure (*softly*) Great happiness, and utter grief. I hear bells ringing, folk singing in the street for joy. Then I hear their tears.

Blankenfeld (*impressed*) When will this be?

Cowled Figure Soon. Very soon . . .

Rollo (*stepping forward*) Please sir . . . what do you see for me?

The Doctor starts forward as if to prevent the Cowled Figure from speaking, but he is too late

Cowled Figure For you? I see a curse that becomes a blessing; and a blessing changed to a curse . . .

Blankenfeld (*hastily*) We must go, Rollo. Thank you, Doctor, and good-bye. Martin . . .

Blankenfeld and Rollo exit

Doctor (*smiling wryly*) Well, Martin, you're like Priam's famous daughter—condemned always to speak the truth, but never to be believed. But perhaps that's a mercy of God as well. Tell me, what do you see for me?

Cowled Figure I see a dark stranger sitting at your table and sharing a plate of Fraulein Krauf's excellent stew!

Doctor (*laughing*) That at least we can make good. Sup with me tonight, old friend. These are dark days for us all, and will grow darker, my very bones know it . . .

The Doctor places an arm affectionately on the Cowled Figure's shoulder, and they leave the stage together as—

The CURTAIN *falls*

A Light comes up on the Narrator

Narrator The Mayor and the Corporation
        Quaked with a mighty consternation.
        They knew the people could vote them out
        Of the office in which they'd got so stout . . .

SCENE 3

A street in Hamelin

On a shadowy, ill-defined stage a group of Children taunt Rollo, the crippled boy. He is in tears. He swings at them unavailingly with his fists and all but overbalances

Children Loppy-legs! Loppy-legs!

At the height of the battle the curious figure of the Piper appears at the back of the stage. He stands in silhoutte, hands on hips, staring down at the Children. He does not speak, but the Children back away in fear. He turns back into the shadows and vanishes as—

the CURTAIN *falls*

SCENE 4

The Council Chamber

There is a long table and five chairs

The Mayor and his Wife are standing by the window, staring down into the street. The Mayor turns aside with irritation

Wife Otto, what was all that noise?

Mayor (*with ill humour*) That crippled son of Blankenfeld's, young Rollo. He's getting to be as big a nuisance as his father. The others had found a frog down by the river. He took it off them, so they turned on him. Some stranger chased them away.

Blankenfeld enters, looking haggard, with Gravell and Schmidt, two other members of the Council

The Council take their places at the table, with the Mayor in the centre and his Wife on his right. The Mayor rises and coughs importantly

Mayor Now, gentlemen, I've called this meeting because it seems to me that events in the town are in danger of getting out of hand. As you know, a herd of commoners actually forced their way in here yesterday and had the insolence to deliver an ultimatum. I don't need to tell you that unless we can come up with some positive proposals our chances of winning the next election are non-existent; but it's also my opinion that if the townsfolk meant a half of what they said we could be in serious trouble long before that. I'll listen to any reasonable suggestion.

Blankenfeld Why don't we do simply as the people asked? Issue free traps and set up a bounty system?

Gravell Because, Blankenfeld, that would cost money. Money! If we're to keep up any sort of municipal standard, we need a few little extras. We simply can't afford it.

Wife Herr Gravell, I do so agree. The common people need standards to look up to. Without them, they'd be lost!

Blankenfeld But money raised by taxing the town isn't ours to

do what we like with. It belongs to Hamelin; it must be used
for the town's good.

Schmidt (*kindly*) Look, old fellow, we all respect this honest
streak of yours, but you can be really tiresome. Everybody
knows this sort of job carries a few perks; I mean—dash it—
if it didn't, who would do it?

Blankenfeld (*bitterly*) Perhaps those with the good of the people
at heart.

Mayor (*hastily*) Now let's not get involved in personality
clashes, or we'll be here all day. If we could get back to the
point of issue . . .

Wife (*silkily*) May I make a suggestion?

Mayor But, of course, my dear. What do you propose?

Wife Couldn't we *pretend* to hire an expert? After all, if he
failed we could say we'd *tried*.

Blankenfeld I hardly think . . .

There is a tap at the door

Mayor (*yelling at the top of his voice*) What is it *now*? *Come in!*

*As he shouts, the Piper enters. He is as Browning described
him: tall and thin, wearing a strange pied costume and with cold,
piercing eyes. He stands in the doorway and nods to the surprised
Council*

Mayor COME IN!

Piper At your service. . . .

Mayor (*visibly flustered at finding the stranger already in the room*)
Er . . . who the Devil are you!

Piper Surely you know me? We've met many times before . . .

Mayor (*angrily*) Met? I've never seen you before in my life!

Piper (*staring coldly*) Perhaps not for a number of years. But no
matter. (*He bows gracefully to the company*) People call me
the Pied Piper.

Gravell (*moving automatically to the attack*) Well, if you've
come up here with another load of complaints, there's nothing
we can do for you. All avenues have been explored.

Schmidt You don't even look like a citizen of Hamelin to me!

Piper I am a citizen of many towns. Hamelin is one of them.

Mayor (*tartly*) Well, you don't dress like it. How dare you come
to our town with your grumbling!

Piper (*softly*) I make no complaint.

Mayor Exactly. How dare you—what? You *haven't* come to complain? What have you come for then?

Piper You have a plague in Hamelin—a plague of rats.

Schmidt Now just a minute, my good fellow. The Sanitary Department's been having a little difficulty, certainly, but you've no right to go about spreading these alarmist reports . . .

Piper (*coldly, expressionlessly*) A plague of rats.

Blankenfeld (*wearily*) Why beat about the bush? We're inundated with the things. It's like the plague the Lord sent Pharaoh. They've just about taken over the town.

Piper This is what I have heard.

Mayor Well, what's it to you anyway? What right have you got to march in here talking about plagues? Did you come to laugh at us?

Piper I came to offer you aid. But I see you do not need it. (*He turns on his heel*) Good day, gentlemen.

Mayor (*hurriedly*) Now, just a minute . . .

<table>
<tr>
<td rowspan="11">Gravell
Schmidt
Mayor
Wife</td>
<td>Aid? How can you offer us aid?</td>
<td rowspan="11">(Speaking together)</td>
</tr>
<tr><td>We've tried everything already . . .</td></tr>
<tr><td>We're at our wits' end. . . .</td></tr>
<tr><td>You experts are so expensive . . .</td></tr>
<tr><td>How can we trust you?</td></tr>
<tr><td>You'll take our money and just clear out!</td></tr>
<tr><td>We've combed the country . . .</td></tr>
<tr><td>Every expert we employ, the rats double numbers.</td></tr>
<tr><td>What can you do?</td></tr>
</table>

The Piper waits patiently and it is Blankenfeld who finally restores quiet

Blankenfeld I . . . apologize for my colleagues, sir. But we have been under strain, under great strain; we are over-wrought. And after so many disappointments we have become desperate. If you really have a solution, we will take it, whatever the cost.

Mayor (*hastily*) Within reason, of course.

Piper If I rid your town of rats, will you give me . . . a thousand
guilders?

*The Council react with amazement and disbelief at what to them is
a very modest demand*

Mayor My dear fellow! A thousand guilders, to lift this living
curse from us! A thousand guilders? We'd pay fifty!

*He laughs uproariously. The other Councillors, with the exception
of Blankenfeld join in. The Mayor waddles towards the Piper with
outstretched hand. The Piper ignores it, but the Mayor is not unduly
put out*

Mayor Well, what method do you hope to use? Traps? Poison?
Got to bear the environment in mind, y'know.
Piper My methods are my own. And your . . . environment will
not be harmed.
Schmidt When do you propose to start?
Piper (*softly*) At once . . .
Mayor (*with a gesture rather like shooting his cuffs*) Well, Mr . . .
Piper, this is the deal then. You make a start . . . *at once* . . .
on this little problem (*winking heavily at his cronies*) and
we'll pay you on completion . . . one thousand guilders. No
cure, no pay, as they say, eh?
Piper (*icily*) Those are my terms.
Mayor (*continuing to find the thing a considerable joke*) Well,
gentlemen, m'dear, I declare this meeting closed. We'll leave
our . . . ah . . . friend to his work, and reconvene in the morning. Agreed?

*The Council, apart from Blankenfeld, rises, muttering general
agreement. They move towards the door*

Schmidt The fellow must be completely off his head . . .
Mayor Oh, quite definitely mad. I like doing business with
him . . .
Wife I hope he's not *dangerous*. There's something of the
anarchist about him.
Gravell If it comes to the worst a spell in the town jail would
soon cool him off . . .

The Council exits

Blankenfeld, still sitting at his place, stares up thoughtfully at the Piper, who crosses to the window and stands looking down gravely into the street

Blankenfeld Well, what do you intend to do? You've taken on a pretty big operation, you know.

The Piper half turns, seemingly lost in thought

It's either trapping or poison . . .

Piper (*softly*) I suppose one might call it poison. The worst poison of all. I shall offer them hope . . .

Blankenfeld (*incredulously*) What?

Piper (*smiling fleetingly*) Hope. The dream of plenty, of safety. Of the life eternal. The greatest snare—for rats as for men . . .

Blankenfeld (*convinced of his ally's powers, but dubious*) Rats don't dream . . .

Piper All that lives, dreams. Your Mayor dreams of palaces of white and gold, of riches beyond counting. You dream of peace and harmony, a land where love is supreme, where children walk straight-limbed. Horses dream of oats and bran; earthworms of the humus of Elysium. And who can number the great green dreams of trees?

Blankenfeld (*still watching narrowly*) And rats?

Piper (*smiling once more*) It's enough. Leave the rats to me . . .

Blankenfeld (*curiously*) What did you mean by telling the Mayor he'd met you before?

Piper He knew me once. They all did. You still do, don't you?

Blankenfeld rises as if half-mesmerized, staring at the Piper. He frowns, trying to recall

(*Very quietly*) He knew me. But he killed me. *Now* do you understand?

The Piper turns to the door, and quietly exits

As Blankenfeld stands, still dazed, the scuffling and squeaking of the Rats is once more heard, followed by a high, sinister laugh. Blankenfeld wakes from his trance with a start. He hurries to the window and stands staring earnestly down, as the Lights fade to a Black-out and—

the CURTAIN *falls*

Scene 5

In the Land of the Rats

The stage is bare and the lighting dim and shadowy

A group of Rats crouches together towards the back of the stage. Throughout the scene their heads weave and bob, throwing dark, distorted shadows across the backdrop. The movement and the closeness of the group suggests the Gestalt brain of the Rats. When the Rats speak, their voices are sibilant and sinister. The Piper stands facing them, a little to one side, hands on hips, smiling sardonically

Piper I have come to offer you Paradise.

1st Rat We have Paradise . . .

Piper Where? I see only houses and people. Dirt and struggle and sudden death.

2nd Rat Look again, stranger. There is plenty.

All Rats (*echoing*) Plenty . . . plenty . . . plenty, plenty.

6th Rat There is plenty . . .

Piper But for how long? Your numbers increase, by the day, by the hour. How can any one place support your squeaking hordes of young?

All Rats Plenty . . . plenty . . .

Piper Soon Hamelin will be empty—a sucked-out husk. Then the dark will come, the long nights of winter. Dark, and the cold. Then you will begin to die . . .

The movement of the Rats becomes more agitated, then subsides again

4th Rat We will move on . . .

3rd Rat There are many towns . . .

All Rats Plenty . . . plenty . . .

5th Rat Many more towns like Hamelin . . .

1st Rat We will eat Hamelin, then we will go . . .

All Rats We will not starve.

Piper (*grimly*) The towns are far away. And the cold is coming. Listen and see . . .

He puts his pipe to his lips, and plays strange music

3rd Rat Ohh . . . Ohh . . .
2nd Rat I see the snow falling, settling on streets and roofs . . .
4th Rat Cold! Cold! My feet are hurting . . .!
1st Rat The air itself is freezing! I can't move!
All Rats Cold . . . Cold. . .!

The trembling of the group becomes very violent indeed

7th Rat It's a trick, I tell you. This man is a conjuror, don't you
listen to him! Stop your ears!

The Piper plays again

1st Rat The vats are empty! We run round and round, but there
is no food! We are starving!
5th Rat The dogs are coming! Hear them padding, down every
street, through every lane. See their eyes!
All Rats Run for your lives!
7th Rat There are no dogs! We have eaten the dogs! It is
summer, there are piles of food! Sniff, brothers, smell the food!
Feel the warm air!
2nd Rat There is death! Death everywhere! Death in the empty
barns, in the streets, in the fields!
1st Rat See the traps, growing through the snow! They fill with
our children! Listen to them! *The traps are alive!*
All Rats Run! Let us flee! For our lives!
7th Rat (*desperately*) Listen to me! When have I lied to you, or
led you falsely? It's all a trick. He's one of the Old Folk, the
People of Faery. That's no pipe; that's a wand! He's be-
witching you . . .
All Rats Flee . . .! Run . . .! For your lives . . .!

*The Piper stops playing, and the terrified clamour of the Rats
ceases. The Piper stands by gravely*

7th Rat (*baring his teeth and snarling*) Very clever, Piper. But
you will not fool me with your trickeries. We two have met
before. And I remember!
Piper I showed you no tricks. I showed the future, as it must
surely be, unless you accept my offer.
7th Rat Don't listen to him! He's lying again!
1st Rat How can we find your Paradise?
Piper It isn't far away. Listen again, and watch.

The Piper puts his pipe to his lips and plays again

1st Rat Ohh, apples and jam!

2nd Rat Sugar and ripe corn!

3rd Rat I taste the flavour of pickles and cheese!

4th Rat And cider! Cider in open casks, clear and golden and strong!

5th Rat Butter! Mountains of creamy, fresh-made butter. Do you not see the salt stand on it?

All Rats (*variously*) Salted butter!
                         Cider and cheese!
                         Pickles!
                         Ripe corn and apples!
                         Jam!

6th Rat There are tubs of fruit, fresh-picked and succulent. Plums and cherries waiting for our teeth!

1st Rat We shall grow fat and sleek!

2nd Rat There are warm stables with fresh straw! There is fresh, clean mountain water. Doors stand open everywhere! Larders gape, cupboards are full!

3rd Rat It must be Heaven!

All Rats (*echoing*) It must be Heaven! Surely, it must be Heaven!

4th Rat Where can we go to find it?

All Rats (*echoing*) Where can we go . . .?

The Piper stops playing

7th Rat It was no more real than the rest! It's death to listen to him!

All Rats Show us the way! Oh, show us the way!

The Group begins to fragment

7th Rat Brothers! Brothers, do not listen!

All Rats (*dreamily*) The way! Show us the way . . .

The Piper begins to play again, and slowly moves off, with the Rats swarming behind him, squeaking excitedly

The 7th Rat remains behind, watching sadly

7th Rat My brothers! Oh, my brothers!

The Lights fade to a Black-out as—

the CURTAIN *falls*

A Light comes up on the Narrator

Narrator You heard as if an army muttered;
And the muttering grew to a grumbling;
And the grumbling grew to a mighty rumbling;
And out of the houses the rats came tumbling.
Great rats, small rats, lean rats, brawny rats.
Brown rats, black rats, grey rats, tawny rats.
Fathers, mothers, uncles, cousins,
Families by tens and dozens,
Brothers, sisters, husbands, wives,
Followed the Piper for their lives.
From street to street he piped advancing,
And step by step they followed dancing,
Until they came to the River Weser . . .

There is a crash of music

SCENE 6

The Market Place

An excited group of Townspeople is gathered, among which can be seen the various characters who appeared in Scene 1

Tall Man I can't believe it. I saw it with my own eyes, and I still can't believe it!

Thin Man (*wonderingly*). They're gone! All of them! We are free!

Angry Lady What's this you are yelling at me? The rats? Where could they go, I ask you?

Tall Man (*jubilantly*) They're gone, dead, drowned. In the river! The Weser!

Big Man I saw them! I was standing right by!

Small Man I was by the river steps, by the wharf. I heard this noise . . .

Big Man A pattering it was, and a rumbling. And this queer piping. It did something to my back hair, I can tell you . . .

Red-faced Man (*joining group*) So what happened then?

Thin Man It was him! The Piper!

Tall Man A rustling and scraping it was, to start with. Then it grew and grew, like a roaring!

Big Man Like a waterfall!

Thin Man (*soberly*) That's what it looked like as well. A waterfall of rats—black, brown, grey, every colour you can imagine.

Big Man Like a carpet! An old rag carpet, flowing out into the docks! Out from all the streets!

Thin Man He just stepped aside when they got to the Weser. He was . . . laughing. Laughing somehow. But he never stopped the piping . . .

Tall Man You could see them for a mile. All the bodies being rolled down by the tide!

Thin Man And now we'll be able to sleep nights. Us, and all our families. The first time for a year! And all because of the Piper!

Angry Lady (*with Teutonic excess of emotion*) God bless him, I say! He's an angel from Heaven!

Red-faced Man Who is he anyway? The Piper? Nobody seems to know the first thing about him!

Small Man Next thing they'll be telling us up at the Town Hall, it was the Mayor in disguise!

There is a shout of laughter

Thin Man I don't know who he was. I've never seen anybody like him before. That yellow and red, and the way he played those pipes! The rats followed as if they couldn't help themselves!

Red-faced Man Do you suppose it *was* the Corporation that hired him?

Angry Lady Never have they done us good yet. For why should they start now? The only one who gives a tinker's damn is Blankenfeld.

Big Man Well, if they did hire him, that's one part of our taxes well spent. Let's give them the benefit of the doubt!

The Cowled Figure enters

Small Man Hello, it's old Doom-a-Minute! What's new in the disaster line, friend?

Cowled Figure Well may you speak of doom. All of you here. The sky is darkening over Hamelin this instant. Can none of you see?

Thin Man You're late on your cue for once, friend. Hamelin's doom has just been lifted. The Weser's already washing it out to sea!

Tall Man It's a bit much, you know! The happiest day in the town's history and old Doom-and-Gloom is still beefing!

More laughter. The Cowled Figure turns away sadly

The Clerk enters

Clerk People of Hamelin! Good people of Hamelin, hear me! The Mayor has decreed that now his steps to eradicate the rats have proved successful, you are to take ladders and poles and knock down all that remains of their nests. Wipe out every trace of them! All carpenters and builders are meanwhile to report to the Town Hall where they will be allocated the most important repair jobs. We want Hamelin looking the best town in Germany again, as it always did!

The Townspeople cheer, rather half-heartedly

Red-faced Man (*raising his voice*) And who's going to pay for it all, I should like to know!

Clerk (*with a grand gesture*) The Corporation. The Mayor has personally opened the reserve coffers!

Red-faced Man That's nice! Then perhaps he'll pay the bill I sent him six months back for patching his roof!

There are various shouts of "And me," "What about my bill for . . ." etc.

Thin Man Where is the Piper anyway? He saved all of us. I want to shake his hand!

Clerk He'll be up at the Town Hall by now, collecting his fee.

Angry Lady Then I hope he has more luck with you pack of skinflints than ever I had!

Cowled Figure I see the Doom now! Oh, I see it clear! God save us! God save Hamelin!

Clerk (*pompously*) I am quite sure the Council will honour its commitments.

Red-faced Man There has to be a first time for everything, I suppose!

Angry Lady If *I* was this Piper, I'd have seen the colour of their money first!

Clerk (*outraged*) Madam! Are you impuging dishonesty on the part of the Council?

Angry Lady I am, my boy, I am. What's your word for it?

More laughter

Red-faced Man (*shouting*) Well, I'm ready to buckle down to it
  for a start. I'm a carpenter. Who needs me first?
Angry Lady Me, me! So many holes my floors have, like
  colanders, they are!
Tall Man What about me? You can't walk in our front bedroom!
Big Man My roof's falling in, just about!

Other voices call "And mine!" etc.

Clerk (*pleased to be able to reassert his authority*) Well, come up
  to the Town Hall then, as I told you. I'll take your names in
  strict rotation.

*There is a general murmur of agreement from the Townspeople and
they all move off, apart from the Thin Man*

Cowled Figure Can they have forgotten so soon? Are their
  memories so short? They've even forgotten the one they
  should be thanking!
Thin Man (*frowning*) The Piper? He'll be paid.
Cowled Figure (*grimly*) He'll be paid all right. The Old Ones
  always are . . .
Thin Man (*starting*) You don't tell me you believe that old
  fashioned stuff, surely? Faeries are for children's books!
Cowled Figure Call them Faeries if you must. There are other
  names. Some call them one thing, some another. Some call
  them Daemons . . .
Thin Man (*briskly*) I'm afraid you're worrying over nothing, as
  usual. Well, I'm off up to the Town Hall to take my place in
  the queue. This is a great day for Hamelin!

The Thin Man exits

Cowled Figure (*bitterly, shaking his head*) A great day, he calls
  it! It's the blackest day in the history of the town . . .

The Lights fade to a Black-out as—

the CURTAIN *falls*

SCENE 7

The Council Chamber

The Council are all present, including the Mayor and his Wife. An air of jolliness and frivolity prevails

Schmidt It's a great day for Hamelin!

Gravell A great day for us!

Wife The townspeople are delighted! Dancing in the streets!

Mayor (*grandly*) And so they should be! You're right, Gravell; we're bound to be re-elected now. Who can stand in our way? Who found this rat-catcher fellow after all and set him to work?

Wife My dear, you're so clever. How could the town do without you now?

Blankenfeld (*stonily*) We did not find him. He came to us. And we all but turned him away.

Gravell Really, Blankenfeld, must you even spoil a day like this?

Schmidt (*aside*) Self-righteousness is the most boring thing . . .

Mayor (*fussily*) Well, we all know Blankenfeld likes pouring cold water . . .

Blankenfeld (*stung*) On the subject of cold water, where's the thousand guilders to come from?

Mayor (*taken aback*) What thousand guilders?

Gravell (*bored*) I suppose he means the money for the wretched Piper.

Mayor Piper? Oh, him . . . I don't want him in here spoiling the celebrations. If he turns up I shall send him packing.

Wife I quite agree, my dear. He's certainly no gentleman. People like that are better off with their own kind.

Gravell Quite right, my dear lady!

Schmidt Well, if there's no reward money to pay, I suppose we can afford a party.

Mayor (*brightening*) Ah! A party! No, a banquet. Let's not be half-hearted. We've got most of the venison left, piles of pastries, that Rhenish. We'll send a cart up for some snow to cool it . . .

Wife There's that suckling pig to roast . . .

Mayor (*warming to his theme*) And meringues and eclairs to follow; honey cakes, scones, chocolate!

Blankenfeld (*rising*) I can't believe what I'm hearing.

Mayor Peanut butter, salted almonds . . . what?

Blankenfeld (*in rising anger*) We entered into solemn agreement with the Piper to pay the fee he asked. Neither more nor less. And he carried out his part of the bargain. He performed a miracle—for coppers!

Gravell It would be an even bigger miracle to bring the rats back though!

Mayor Precisely. So he isn't in a very good position for bargaining, is he?

Schmidt See, Blankenfeld, his worship has thought of everything!

As Blankenfeld stands, appalled and at a loss for words, there is a tap at the door. The Piper enters. An embarrassed silence falls, broken at last by the Piper

Piper Well, gentlemen, I believe we have a little transaction to complete.

The silence lengthens, and the Piper shows signs of impatience

Gentlemen, the rats are destroyed. I have fulfilled my promise.

Mayor Er . . . yes, and very ably, very ably indeed. The town is most grateful. I . . . er . . . we were considering in fact a small celebration. We'd be delighted if you would join us . . .

Piper (*gravely*) I thank you, but that will not be possible. I have a pressing engagement in the Middle East.

Wife The where?

Mayor *The Middle East*, dear. Rather a long way off. Well, we mustn't detain you, Mr . . . er . . . Piper. Some other time perhaps. Thank you and . . . er . . . good-bye. (*He holds his hand out, but the Piper shows no inclination to move*)

Piper First, if you please, my thousand guilders.

Schmidt A thousand guilders! You must be joking!

Gravell Where would we find that sort of money? We're only a poor town!

Schmidt (*clicking his tongue*) A thousand guilders. Well, well . . .

Mayor I don't think I quite understand . . .

Piper (*coldly*) You understand perfectly well. I have come for the fee agreed between us.

During the remainder of this scene the lights dim to the same level as in the Rat scene, and the Mayor and Councillors, moving together, take up the same attitudes as the Rats took. Only Blankenfeld remains standing apart

Mayor It isn't my custom to be heckled by vagabonds like you . . .

Piper And it isn't *my* custom to ask twice for my dues!

Schmidt What do you mean by that?

Gravell (*amused*) I almost believe the fellow's trying to threaten us!

Blankenfeld (*desperately*) I'm sure there's been some mistake . . . I'll pay the money myself. I can still realize a little cash. If you would give me a day, two at the outside . . .

The Piper turns to him with a look almost of compassion

Piper Let the world pay for its own sins, Blankenfeld. You cannot absolve them . . .

Mayor (*fumbling in his purse*) Look, we don't want you to think hard of us. A thousand guilders is a ridiculous amount; everybody knew we were joking. Here's fifty. Be satisfied with that, and think yourself lucky! (*He throws down the coins, but the Piper makes no attempt to pick them up*)

Piper Then you deny the agreement we made?

Mayor (*blustering*) Yes, I deny it! We all deny it!

Schmidt Take the fifty, Piper. It's the best offer you'll get.

Gravell The deal between us ended at the river bank. What's dead can't be brought to life can it?

Mayor There was no agreement! And that's our last word!

Blankenfeld You know there was! Have you all gone mad?

Gravell Keep *out* of these financial matters, Blankenfeld. You know they only confuse you.

Blankenfeld It isn't a matter of finance, it's a matter of honour!

Wife I don't think you should offer this man money, Herr Blankenfeld. You'll only encourage his greed.

Blankenfeld Greed!

Gravell (*firmly*) Greed. And I for one have no intention of knuckling under to blackmail!

Blankenfeld This man saved our town! Now we refuse his dues! What sort of people are we? How can we ever raise our heads again?

Schmidt What sort of people are we? We're shrewd people, that's what we are. Stop crawling, Blankenfeld, for God's sake.

Mayor That's right, Blankenfeld. You're snivelling. Makes me sick! (*To the Piper*) As for you, you just clear out. And think yourself lucky you're getting out with a whole skin. Go on, take yourself away! Go and blow your pipe till you burst!

Piper (*slowly and without emotion*) That is your final word? (*He reads his answer in their faces, and bows slightly*) Then, so be it . . .

Blankenfeld Piper, for the sake of God . . . whatever you're planning . . . don't!

Piper (*turning to him*) You, Blankenfeld, I exempt from the doom this town has brought upon itself. For the rest of you, Mr Mayor, Frau Burgomeister, Herr Schmidt, Herr Gravell . . . for the sake of a thousand guilders, Hamelin will remember me a thousand years. A year for every guilder.

The Piper exits

The Lights come up again slowly, and the Council turn to face one another; for a moment there is silence

Mayor Well, that's over with then. Nasty business, rather . . . (*He cracks his knuckles and beams round*) Now to business . . . What form should the celebrations take? Remember, it isn't far to election time. We shall want maximum coverage.

Blankenfeld (*unable to contain himself any longer*) You disgust me! The whole pack of you! You're worse than the criminals in the town gaol!

Wife Criminals!

Blankenfeld (*leaping up*) Criminals I said and criminals I mean! Sitting calmly round a table, talking of celebrations! You cheated that man, you've cheated the town. And it'll be the town that has to pay!

Gravell Sit down, you tiresome fellow. You really are overwrought.

Schmidt The fellow's raving like a madman!

Blankenfeld A madman is just what I am—mad to talk of principles to those who have none! Mad to even think of decency and fair play in this—*rats' nest*!

Mayor (*enraged*) *Sit down, sir!*

Blankenfeld I will not sit down! (*His voice rises uncontrollably*) Answer me one thing: have any of you seen that fellow before? Do any of you know where he comes from? What he is? We've seen a miracle performed before our eyes. Now, with your grubbing for pennies, you've enraged him. What will his pipes call next, do you suppose? Our chickens? (*Distraught, he runs for the door*) I've got to find him ... there might still be a way ...

Blankenfeld runs out

Mayor (*shouting after him*) Judas!

Wife What an outburst! What's happened to old-fashioned manners these days? That's what I'd like to know!

Schmidt Quite appalling. I only hope he doesn't run all over the town telling tales to all and sundry. He could totally ruin our image!

Mayor (*suddenly thoughtful*) You have a point there, Schmidt. He was certainly wildly excited—hardly rational. I think perhaps we better have a word with the Constable. I think our friend would be best restrained; for his own good, of course. We can let him out again when the fuss dies down.

Gravell Like after the elections.

Schmidt I agree. We certainly don't want him upsetting the party!

Mayor (*going to the door*) Orb, come in for a minute, will you?

The Clerk enters

Clerk Yes, sir?

Mayor Orb, get hold of the Town Constable at once. He's to arrest Herr Blankenfeld and hold him till further notice. And tell him to be discreet!

Clerk Herr Blankenfeld!

Mayor Don't stand there gaping, you great oaf! Herr Blankenfeld is sick. There's no time to lose.

Clerk At once, Your Honour.

The Clerk turns to leave, but stands still in surprise, as do the Council, as the faint but clear sound of pipe music is heard

Gravell (*in alarm*) That damned magician again! What's he think he's up to this time?

Wife Listen! I can hear children's voices. I can hear laughter.

Schmidt I expect they're laughing at the fellow's absurd dress!
Wife Well, I can only hope our little Heidi isn't among them. I don't like the idea of her mixing with commoners' brats.
Clerk Shall I go for the Constable now, sir?
Mayor Yes, yes. Be quick about it. And don't forget—discretion!
Clerk I'll tell him, Your Worship. Depend on me!

The Clerk exits

Gravell What *is* that row? It's getting louder all the time. You can hardly hear yourself think!

The door bursts open and the Clerk rushes in, dishevelled and panic-stricken

Clerk The children! Oh, sir, the children!
Mayor Are you mad? How dare you burst in like this? What children?
Clerk I couldn't . . . get out—out of the building. They . . . it was like a river, sir. The street was full. All laughing they were and skipping and running . . . after him, sir—the Piper! All the children of the town!

There is a moment of frozen surprise. Then the Mayor drops back heavily into his chair, his face a blank, his hands on its arms

Mayor The children!
Gravell He must be stopped. Call out the Guard!
Schmidt My son must be out there!

Schmidt rushes out

Wife Heidi! My Heidi!

The Mayor's Wife runs out distractedly, followed by the Mayor

Gravell slowly puts his head in his hands

Gravell What have we done, Orb? In God's name, what have we done?

The Lights fade to a Black-out as—

the CURTAIN *falls*

A Light comes up on the Narrator

Narrator All the little boys and girls
With rosy cheeks and flaxen curls,
And sparkling eyes and teeth like pearls,
Tripping and skipping, ran merrily after
The wonderful music, with shouting and
laughter . . .

SCENE 8

The Town Square

There is much shouting and disorder. A mob of bewildered Towns-people is milling about, including the Thin Man and the Angry Lady. The Cowled Figure is standing apart

Blankenfeld enters

Blankenfeld (*shouting*) Stop him! For the love of God, stop him! Don't let him take them away! (*He grabs the Thin Man, who is standing nearby*) He's taking them away!

Thin Man Calm down, Herr Blankenfeld, you're beside yourself. Who are you talking about? And what's he taking away?

Blankenfeld They're following—like the rats. Can't you hear them?

Thin Man I can hear a lot of children. They seem to be having a grand time.

Blankenfeld (*sobbing for breath*) They wouldn't pay him! The Council wouldn't pay! He said he'd be revenged. He said we'd remember a thousand years!

Thin Man (*in dawning horror*) *The children!* Quick, you! And you! To the gates—head him off!

Blankenfeld We must try to head him off!

The Thin Man and Blankenfeld exit, leaving the citizens staring. The Cowled Figure joins the group

Angry Lady (*in tears*) But for why should he take the children? Who would harm the children?

Cowled Figure Did I not warn you? And did you not refuse to heed? Now you have cheated the Old Ones. This is their answer.

Angry Lady I shall wake up. I'm dreaming, that's what it is. I shall wake up soon.

Cowled Figure It's too late to wake. Too late for you all . . .

Angry Lady But I don't understand . . .

Cowled Figure The Old Ones understand. But they do not think as we small mortals think . . .

Angry Lady (*bursting out afresh*) Pity! Have pity on the children!

Cowled Figure (*shaking his head slowly*) In their world there is no pity. Talk of pity to the midday sun; preach to the rolling stars. They know neither pity nor anger. Necessity rules all. The flower dies, the wheel turns . . . a church collapses on the heads of the faithful, and we cry to the Lord for pity. We think it is unfair. But the Old Ones know.

The Tall Man enters, looking dazed

Tall Man I saw it. I saw it all——

All What happened?

Tall Man They were streaming through the gates before we got there. We tried to speak to them, but they didn't seem to hear . . .

The Big Man enters

Big Man They were dancing and singing. Their faces, they were so happy . . .

The Small Man enters

Small Man Some of us tried to touch them, hold them back. But we couldn't . . .

Tall Man It was like a force, something that brushed you aside . . .

Small Man I saw my Pieter among them. I called to him—"Pieter!" I called, "Pieter, what are you doing? Where are you going?" But he . . . never even looked my way. (*He put his face in his hands*)

Big Man I saw *him*, the Piper, head and shoulders above the rest, still playing . . . I couldn't get to him . . .

Angry Lady Where did they go? Where did they *go*?

Tall Man They turned aside. At the river. At first I thought . . . But they climbed the hill, the Koppelberg. That was when it happened . . .

Big Man All the doors of all the rich houses flew open. And their children came out too . . .

Tall Man I saw the Mayor's little girl. . . .

Big Man They were both trying to hold her back . . .

Small Man (*speaking fitfully*) He ran up to the Piper—the Herr Burgomeister—I saw him—he tried to grab his shoulder and his hand went through! Straight through him! *As if he wasn't there at all——*

Angry Lady But where did they go? They couldn't climb the Koppelberg . . .

Small Man I . . . didn't see any more. I daren't look. I ran back here . . .

Angry Lady Our children! Our children!

The Mayor and his Wife enter with Blankenfeld

The Townspeople fall quiet, wonderingly, but the Mayor moves to the centre of the stage like a man in a daze, without even noticing them

Mayor I . . . pleaded with him. Everything I had I offered—my house, my money, my life. I ran after him, but he didn't turn. Just stared ahead, straight ahead, and played that cursed pipe. And then I put my hand out, tried to take his sleeve. Oh, Blankenfeld, she's gone! Our daughter! Heidi's gone——

Blankenfeld (*grief-stricken, but solicitous*) You've had a bad fall, Herr Burgomeister. See, you've hurt your leg. (*Steering him*) Come and sit over here. And you, madam.

Schmidt and the Red-faced Man enter

Schmidt I had a son. One son. Straight limbed he was and flaxen haired . . . God! Why didn't we pay? Why did we cheat him? For a thousand guilders . . .

Red-faced Man I had a daughter. Young she was, and fresh as April rain. Her laugh through the house was like a mountain beck. Now the Koppelberg has her. She was all to me, and she's gone. *Why did you not pay?*

Wife (*raising her head*) Heidi! I want my child!

All (*with wailing voices*) Our children! We want our children . . .

The voices slowly fade and with them the lighting on the stage as—

the CURTAIN *falls*

SCENE 9

The Summit of the Koppelberg

To one side there is a shaft of golden light in front of a "magic" doorway. Shadowy children are skipping hand in hand. They pass into the light and vanish through the "magic" doorway

On the other side, the Piper stands playing on a small raised area

> *As the last of the children disappear, Rollo hobbles on. The Piper puts out a hand to restrain him*

Piper Not you, son of Blankenfeld.

Rollo (*desperately*) Please, sir, please, let me go in. Oh, sir, don't stop me now.

Piper (*gravely*) It is not for you, Rollo.

Rollo (*close to tears*) But, sir, the land I saw—the beautiful land. When the music played. There were trees made of music, and fields and hills. I see them still.

The Piper descends from his perch slowly, and smiles

Piper You see the Koppelberg, Rollo. That is all.

Rollo But, sir, that can't be. Look at the golden sunlight. And my friends in there, all laughing. My leg would be cured; the music promised me!

Piper Promises are not always what they seem. Promises are not the law by which men live. That has another, sharper name— necessity. One day you will understand.

The Cowled Figure appears on the other side of the stage

Piper There is one who will take you to your father. Good-bye, Rollo. Be of good cheer.

The Piper moves towards the "magic" doorway

As the Cowled Figure crosses the stage to the boy, Rollo calls out, holding up his arms

Rollo Sir! Sir, will I ever see you again?

The Piper turns back

Piper Understand rightly, my son, and I will never leave you.

Rollo (*desperately*) Sir, who are you?
Piper (*gravely*) I am Conscience, Rollo. Your conscience and the conscience of every man in Hamelin. Never forget me again.

The Piper ducks through the "magic" doorway. There is a roaring noise as of rock grinding, and the golden light is extinguished

Rollo and the Cowled Figure stand together, heads bowed, on an empty stage as the Lights slowly dim and—

the CURTAIN *slowly falls*

FURNITURE AND PROPERTY LIST

Only minimum props are listed here. Additional furnishings may be
used at the Director's discretion.

SCENE 1

On stage: High desk. *On it:* papers, ink-pot
        Chair
        Hat-stand. *On it:* Mayor's hat and cloak
        Quill pen **(Clerk)**
Off stage: Carter's leather apron **(Big Man)**
        Piece of paper **(Red-faced Man)**

SCENE 2

On stage: Desk
        2 chairs
        Pot of ointment **(Doctor)**
Off stage: Crutch **(Rollo)**
        Basket of herbs **(Cowled Figure)**
        Bag of cakes **(Rollo)**

SCENE 4

On stage: Long table
        5 chairs

Scene 5

Personal: Pipe **(Piper)**

SCENE 7

As Scene 4
Personal: Pipe **(Piper)**

SCENE 9

On stage: Small platform for Piper
Personal: Pipe **(Piper)**

LIGHTING PLOT

Property fittings required: nil
Various simple interior and exterior settings

To open: Dim overall lighting

Cue 1	When ready *Light up narrator downstage*	(Page 1)
Cue 2	**Narrator**: "In fifty different sharps and flats." *Bring up lighting in Town Clerk's Office*	(Page 1)
Cue 3	**Narrator**: "...came flocking..." *Fade Light on Narrator*	(Page 1)
Cue 4	**Blankenfeld**: "...I'll help you with those papers ..." *Fade to Black-out*	(Page 8)
Cue 5	When ready *Light up on Narrator downstage*	(Page 9)
Cue 6	**Narrator**: "...for ever stumble, lame?" *Fade Light on Narrator*	(Page 9)
Cue 7	As Scene 2 opens *Lights up on Doctor's Surgery*	(Page 9)
Cue 8	**Doctor**: "...my very bones know it ..." *Fade to Black-out*	(Page 12)
Cue 9	When ready *Light up on Narrator downstage*	(Page 12)
Cue 10	**Narrator**: "...in which they'd got so stout ..." *Fade Light on Narrator*	(Page 12)
Cue 11	As Scene 3 opens *Bring up Street lighting—dim, shadowy*	(Page 12)
Cue 12	As Piper vanishes into shadows *Black-out*	(Page 12)
Cue 13	As Scene 4 opens *Bring up full lighting for Council Chamber*	(Page 13)

EFFECTS PLOT

MADE AND PRINTED IN GREAT BRITAIN BY
LATIMER TREND COMPANY LTD PLYMOUTH
MADE IN ENGLAND

www.ingramcontent.com/pod-product-compliance
Ingram Content Group UK Ltd.
Pitfield, Milton Keynes, MK11 3LW, UK
UKHW020038170726
7214IPUK00036B/259